The Li

of Quotations on

Transformational Change

By Wayne Visser

Paperback edition published in 2018
by Kaleidoscope Futures, London, UK.

Cover photography and design by Wayne Visser.

Printing and distribution by Lulu.com.

ISBN 978-1-908875-99-0

Non-fiction Books by Wayne Visser

Beyond Reasonable Greed: Why Sustainable
   Business is a Much Better Idea!

South Africa: Reasons to Believe

Corporate Citizenship in Africa: Lessons from
   the Past, Paths to the Future

Business Frontiers: Social Responsibility,
   Sustainable Development and Economic
   Justice

The A to Z of Corporate Social Responsibility: A
   Complete Reference Guide to Concepts,
   Codes and Organisations

Making A Difference: Purpose-Inspired
   Leadership for Corporate Sustainability &
   Responsibility

Landmarks for Sustainability

The Top 50 Sustainability Books

The World Guide to CSR: A Country by
   Country Analysis of Corporate Sustainability
   and Responsibility

The Age of Responsibility: CSR 2.0 and the New
   DNA of Business

The Quest for Sustainable Business: An Epic
  Journey in Search of Corporate
  Responsibility

Corporate Sustainability & Responsibility: An
  Introductory Text on CSR Theory & Practice
  – Past, Present & Future

CSR 2.0: Transforming Corporate Sustainability
  and Responsibility

Disrupting the Future: Great Ideas for Creating
  a Much Better World

This is Tomorrow: Artists for a Sustainable
  Future

Sustainable Frontiers: Unlocking Change
  Through Business, Leadership and
  Innovation

The CSR International Research Compendium:
  Volumes 1-3

The World Guide to Sustainable Enterprise:
  Volumes 1-4

The Little Book of Quotations on Social
  Responsibility

The Little Book of Quotations on Sustainable
  Business

Fiction Books by Wayne Visser

About the Author

Dr Wayne Visser is Professor of Integrated Value and holds the Chair in Sustainable Transformation at Antwerp Management School. He is Director of the think-tank and media company, Kaleidoscope Futures and Fellow at Cambridge University's Institute for Sustainability Leadership. His work as a strategy analyst, sustainability advisor, CSR expert, futurist and professional speaker has taken him to over 70 countries in the past 20 years. Dr Visser is author of 28 books – including *Sustainable Frontiers: Unlocking Change Through Business, Leadership and Innovation*. Dr Visser has been recognised as a top 100 thought-leader in trustworthy business and received the Global CSR Excellence & Leadership Award. He founded CSR International, after obtaining a PhD in corporate social responsibility. He previously served as Director of Sustainability Services for KPMG and Strategy Analyst for Capgemini in South Africa. Dr Visser lives in Cambridge, UK.

Website: www.waynevisser.com

Email: wayne@waynevisser.com

"Change is often like an epidemic - it starts slowly, but when it reaches the steep part of the S-curve, watch out!"

From: Beyond Reasonable Greed

"There is a palpable tension between the realities of today and the possibilities of tomorrow"

From: Sustainable Frontiers

"Social and ethical
champions promote
causes based on their
values and beliefs, despite
the personal and
professional risks"

From: The A to Z of Corporate Social Responsibility

"Over-specialisation
eventually leads to
extinction, as we lose our
general adaptability to
deal with change"

From: The Top 50 Sustainability Books

"Capitalism creates instability in the markets and those that suffer the most from this volatility are always the most vulnerable"

From: The Age of Responsibility

"The world has this nasty
habit of changing without
our permission"

From: Disrupting the Futures

"We must find ways to let go of an industrial system that has served us well, but is no longer fit for purpose"

From: Sustainable Frontiers

"Business is a playground
for creativity when it
provides stimulating and
challenging work"

From: Personal Diaries

"Change is all about
connection. In other
words, connectivity is the
underlying catalyst for
change"

From: Sustainable Frontiers

"Magic is the revelation
that results from a
profound change in
perception"

From: Beyond Reasonable Greed

"Unlocking change is not
only about what you do,
but also whether you are
tapped into your own
power"

From: Sustainable Frontiers

"Be inspired to find your own threshold of dynamic tension, and join in the search for creative solutions"

From: Business Frontiers

"We often find that we are no longer the agents of change, but rather its victims"

From: Disrupting the Future

"Without innovation, we are unlikely solve many of our global social and environmental problems"

From: Sustainable Frontiers

"We must constantly shapeshift, liberating ourselves from the old form that defined and constrained us in the past"

From: Beyond Reasonable Greed

"The dying metaphor of
business as a 'rational
machine' must transform
into business as a 'living
whole'"

From: Business Frontiers

"We must learn to let go of cherished ideologies that are causing destruction"

From: Sustainable Frontiers

"Companies are part of the
chain of living organisms -
endowed with life,
personality and evolution"

From: Personal Diaries

"Those that have the foresight to change fundamentally are more likely to survive and thrive"

From: Sustainable Frontiers

"The good news is that
resilience can be learned
and planned for in
advance"

From: Disrupting the Future

"We must learn to let go of beliefs about ways to tackle problems that are failing to resolve crises"

From: Sustainable Frontiers

"Amidst whirlwind changes, many companies operate on high alert, in a permanent state of emergency response"

From: Beyond Reasonable Greed

"First, we must change our
collective minds – and
only then will we change
our collective behaviour"

From: Sustainable Frontiers

"The reductionistic,
mechanistic view of reality
fails to recognise the
synergies in the world
around and within us"

From: Business Frontiers

"We would rather trust (and fight to protect) the present we know than gamble on the future we don't know"

From: Sustainable Frontiers

"Most companies are already in hot water - perhaps mistaking the cooking pot for a jacuzzi?"

From: Beyond Reasonable Greed

"People need to feel the heat: directly, personally, here and now. That might mean lighting a few fires"

From: Sustainable Frontiers

"Each time the world changes, humanity is forced to let go of some of its most cherished beliefs"

From: Beyond Reasonable Greed

"What does the future hold? The sustainable technology innovation wave is only just building"

From: Sustainable Frontiers

"Size, strength or physical agility are seldom the best survival qualities (remember the dinosaurs?)"

From: Business Frontiers

"Many of the World Economic Forum's top 10 most promising technologies have a clear environmental and social focus"

From: Sustainable Frontiers

"Resilience is not a
strategy, but an ability –
one which is shaped and
tempered in the fire of
extreme experience"

From: Disrupting the Future

"Shifting our habits,
attitudes, beliefs and
values is the real secret to
making change happen"

From: Sustainable Frontiers

"For companies that wish to endure – to be literally sustainable – adaptation is the key"

From: Beyond Reasonable Greed

"The best available sustainable technology is not always the most applicable, especially in developing countries"

From: Sustainable Frontiers

"Being in business today is a chaotic and confusing place – a lot like falling down Alice in Wonderland's rabbit hole"

From: Beyond Reasonable Greed

"Business frontiers are the points of tension inherent in current models of business and capitalism"

From: Business Frontiers

"As human beings, our lives are all about change – about growth and development and making things better"

From: Sustainable Frontiers

"Strategies for resilience in times of disruptive change are to: defend, diversify, decentralize, dematerialize and define"

From: Disrupting the Future

"Technology presents citizens with far greater opportunities to engage with sustainability issues than ever before"

From: Sustainable Frontiers

"Shapeshifting means morphing into a completely new being, with new characteristics and potential for the future"

From: Beyond Reasonable Greed

"Scaling the number of networked relationships is at the heart of change, including biological and social evolution"

From: Sustainable Frontiers

"Environmental
champions use their
power, knowledge and
influence to promote an
environmental agenda"

From: The A to Z of Corporate Social Responsibility

"Resistance to change comes from inertia – and inertia happens because change is like an iceberg"

From: Sustainable Frontiers

"When business fails to see the long-term effect of gradual changes, it displays classic boiled frog syndrome"

From: Beyond Reasonable Greed

"Not only is technological innovation booming, but it is rapidly shifting towards sustainable solutions"

From: Sustainable Frontiers

"Remember that evolution also happens in great leaps of sudden transformation, so-called discontinuities"

From: Beyond Reasonable Greed

"If we are to survive (let alone thrive), the world is going to have to change – dramatically, radically and irreversibly"

From: Sustainable Frontiers

"Change happens! And we are left somewhere between mildly irritated and battling for our very survival"

From: Disrupting the Future

"Impacts that are far away, or in the future, are like smouldering fires in the distance: not action-worthy"

From: Sustainable Frontiers

"Forget quarterly; companies are going to need to learn what it means to survive epochs and symbolic ice ages"

From: Beyond Reasonable Greed

"Revolutionary change is more often the result of new ways of thinking than new ways of doing"

From: Sustainable Frontiers

"The greatest creativity -

in nature, humans,

organisations and society –

happens when different

fields overlap"

From: Beyond Reasonable Greed

"The sustainability
revolution is as much
about changing
perceptions, attitudes and
behaviours as changing
technology"

From: Sustainable Frontiers

"Faced with the changes and challenges ahead, the skill of shapeshifting is going to be indispensable to companies"

From: Beyond Reasonable Greed

"The decline of civilizations starts with the failure to open the public and political mind to new possibilities"

From: Sustainable Frontiers

"A lesson from nature for business leaders and economists: if one variable is maximised, the system becomes rigid and collapses"

From: Business Frontiers

"If we want real transformation in society, our best chance is to keep spinning the wheel of systems change"

From: Sustainable Frontiers

"The best chance for companies to survive change is to develop a better understanding of how evolution itself works"

From: Beyond Reasonable Greed

"The future is uncertain –
and our greatest fear as
humans is a fear of the
unknown"

From: Sustainable Frontiers

"The universe and society as a rational, mechanical construct is giving way to a new, creative, holistic understanding"

From: Beyond Reasonable Greed

"Use blue skies to create
the reasons to change,
baby steps for momentum
and big beliefs to sustain
energy"

From: Sustainable Frontiers

"Being resilient is about adapting when everything around us is changing – the way an aspen forest copes with an avalanche"

From: Disrupting the Future

"Contrary to what some may think, emerging markets cannot be assumed to lag on sustainable technological innovation"

From: Sustainable Frontiers

"We are living through a
time of profound change
and no more so than in the
business arena"

From: Beyond Reasonable Greed

"Sustainable technologies are transforming our outdated industrial model, which is no longer fit for purpose"

From: Sustainable Frontiers

"Economies and businesses that constantly strive for unlimited growth are sowing the seeds of our collective destruction"

From: Business Frontiers

"When it comes to reinventing capitalism, eco-innovation is one of the next waves business will want to surf"

From: Sustainable Frontiers

"Now, the formerly mute public citizen has an amplified voice through technology-enabled networking"

From: Beyond Reasonable Greed

"We are scared to let go,
because we are
comfortable clinging to
our consumptive habits
and selfish behaviours"

From: Sustainable Frontiers

"The secret to transformational change in the world is connectivity and dexterity"

From: Disrupting the Future

"Civilizations that fail to
change are civilizations
that ultimately fall"

From: Sustainable Frontiers

"We need to do much more if we are to reverse the 'trickle-up' economics that is hard-wired into our Western capitalist system"

From: The Quest for Sustainable Business

"People become trapped
in a paradigm - a pattern
of thinking - and are
closed to a different,
emergent world-view"

From: Sustainable Frontiers

"Most companies have a very poor radar system for detecting and responding to threats that build slowly over time"

From: Beyond Reasonable Greed

"We will all have to let go
of cherished beliefs and
strategies that are not
working"

From: Sustainable Frontiers

"By pursing resilience strategies, we will be much better placed to endure the creative destruction to come"

From: Disrupting the Future

"When change does turn our lives upside down (as it will), how can we become more resilient?"

From: Sustainable Frontiers

"By maximising profits
and growth, business and
the economy inevitably
creates systemic
malfunctioning in other
areas"

From: Business Frontiers

"Learning only happens
when synapses are
formed: they connect the
neurons to each other"

From: Sustainable Frontiers

"Businesses struggle to distinguish between short-term storms and the long-term trend of a climate that's changing"

From: Beyond Reasonable Greed

"If we want to save the sustainability movement, we will have to get much smarter about change"

From: Sustainable Frontiers

"The world is changing so fast that only a company with the adaptability and resourcefulness of a fox will survive"

From: Beyond Reasonable Greed

"If there is one reason why organisational change fails, it is because we underestimate resistance to change"

From: Sustainable Frontiers

"There are many threats that could boil the corporate toads, from creeping income inequality to climate change"

From: Beyond Reasonable Greed

"As humans, we are always 'chasing the blue' – so we have to be convinced that where we are going is sunnier"

From: Sustainable Frontiers

"In a world of increasingly volatile sustainability challenges, resilience strategies can dramatically increase our survival chances"

From: Disrupting the Future

"If you're trying to make
change happen, use
burning platforms to
create the urgency for
change"

From: Sustainable Frontiers

"As a global society, we desperately need to create a new mythology to guide and inspire our collective psyche"

From: Beyond Reasonable Greed

"The first step to overcoming short-termism is to challenge the prevailing wisdom"

From: Sustainable Frontiers

"The rules of the game are
changing in radical ways
that will make cherished
business thinking and
practices obsolete"

From: Beyond Reasonable Greed

"Eco-innovation is the next evolution beyond eco-efficiency, to strategically transform the whole business model"

From: Sustainable Frontiers

"The current model
driving business has
outlived its usefulness"

From: Beyond Reasonable Greed

"Necessity, rather than an unexpected attack on conscience, will drive the transition to a circular economy"

From: Sustainable Frontiers

"Organisations that fail to transform into more holistic entities will be those which have failed to adapt and will die"

From: Business Frontiers

"More patents have been filed in the past 5 years than the previous 30 for climate change mitigation technologies"

From: Sustainable Frontiers

"Mathematicians know well that dynamic systems often go non-linear after a tipping point is reached"

From: Beyond Reasonable Greed

"If we fail to achieve a
sustainable technology
revolution, we will face
'overshoot and collapse' as
a civilization"

From: Sustainable Frontiers

"In change, the tipping point is always a relatively small number, substantially less than the expected 50 percent"

From: Beyond Reasonable Greed

"The challenges of the 21st century will stretch our collective capacity for innovation like never before"

From: Sustainable Frontiers

---

www.ingramcontent.com/pod-product-compliance
Lightning Source LLC
Chambersburg PA
CBHW060626210326
41520CB00010B/1491